The Cake

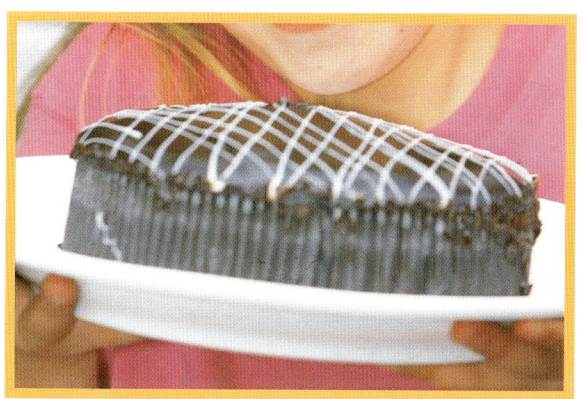

words by Josephine Croser
photographs by Russell Millard

The cake is in a shop.

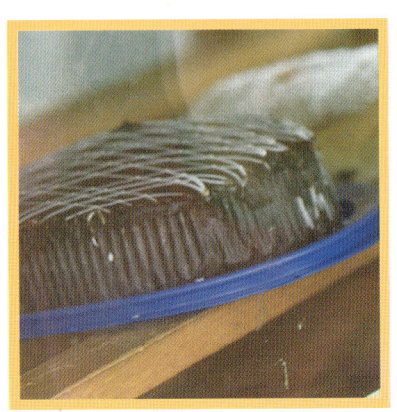

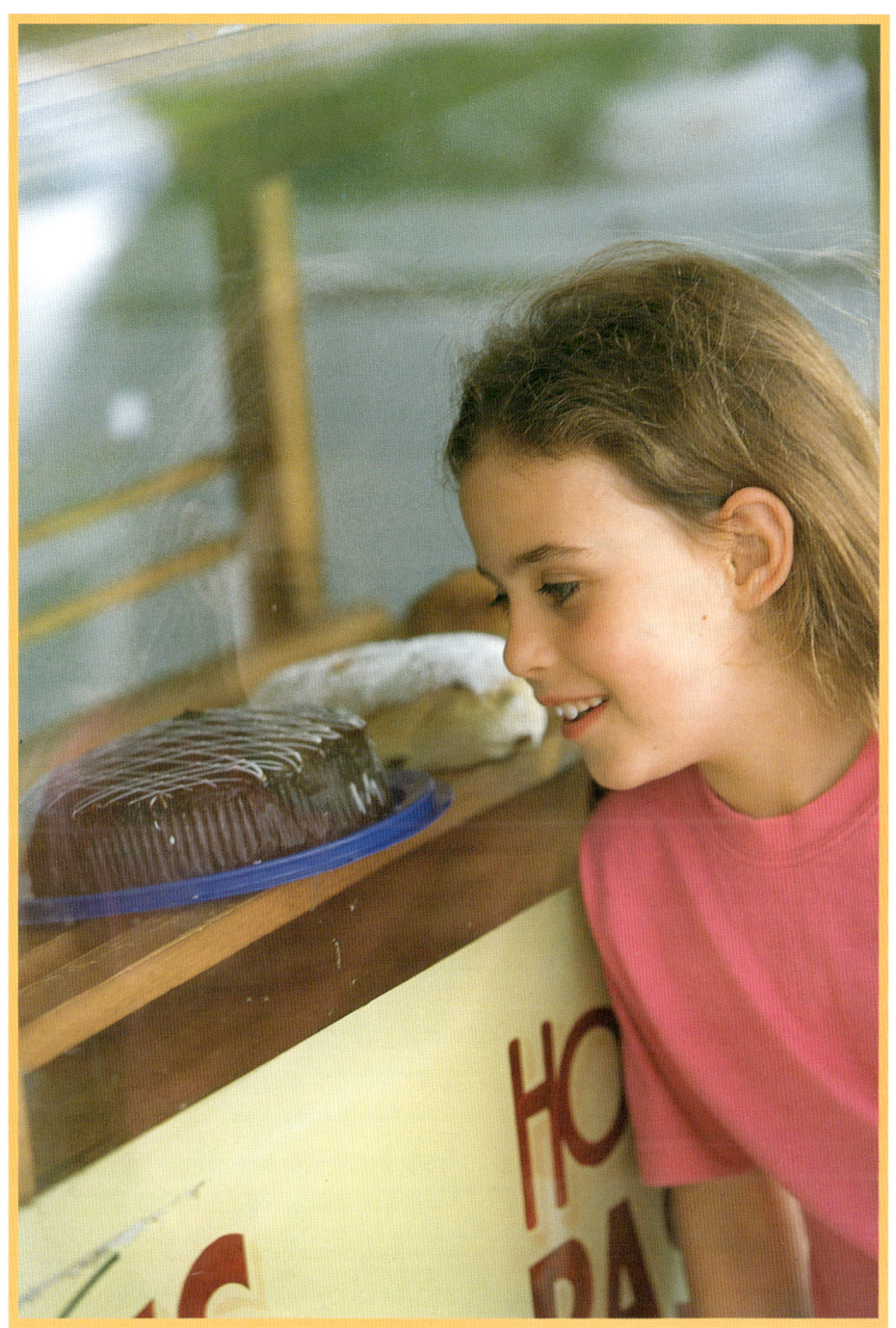

The cake is in a box.

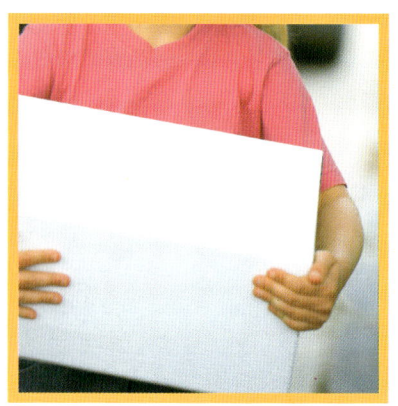

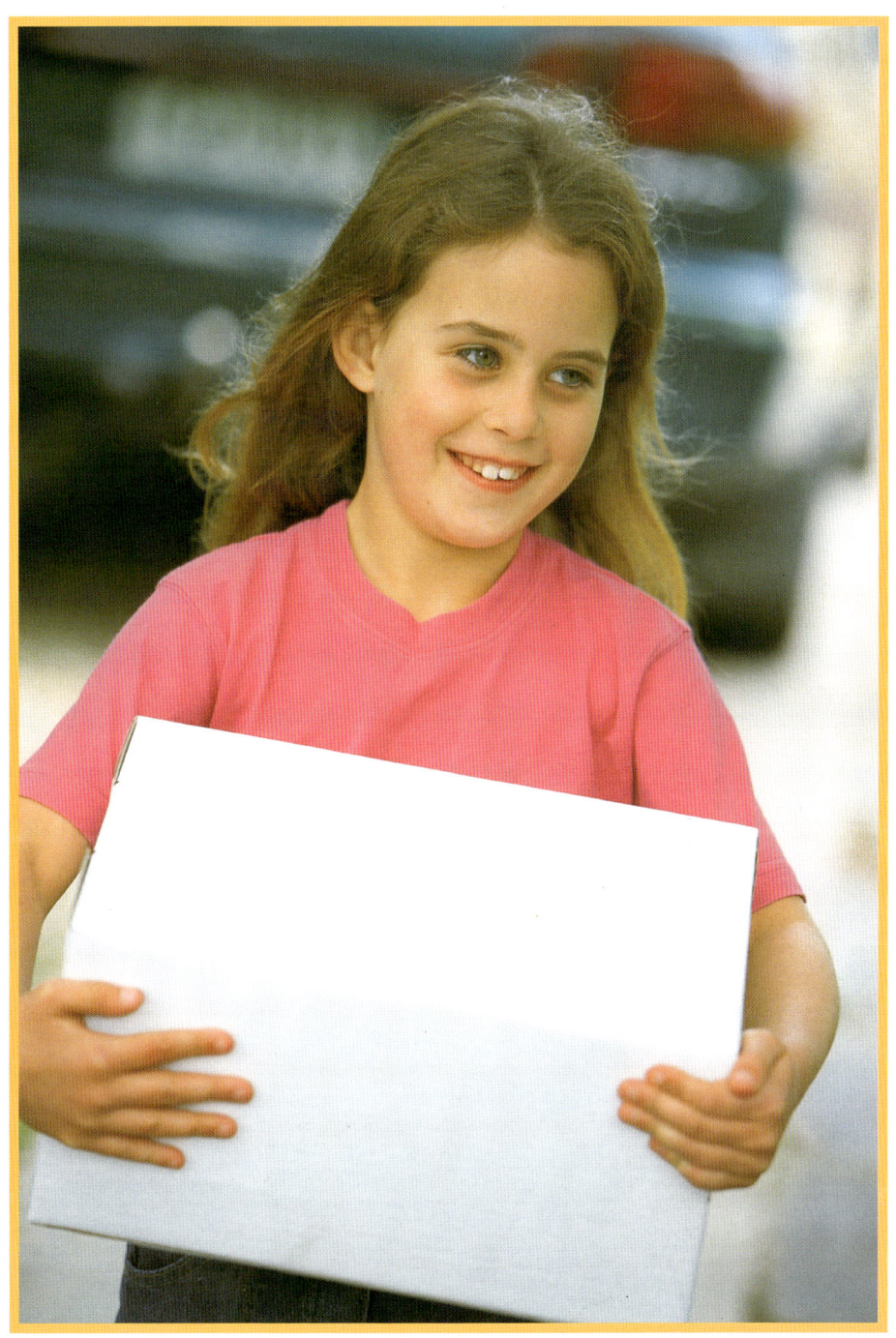

The box is in a bag.

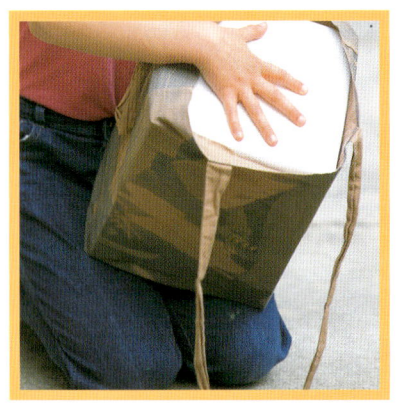

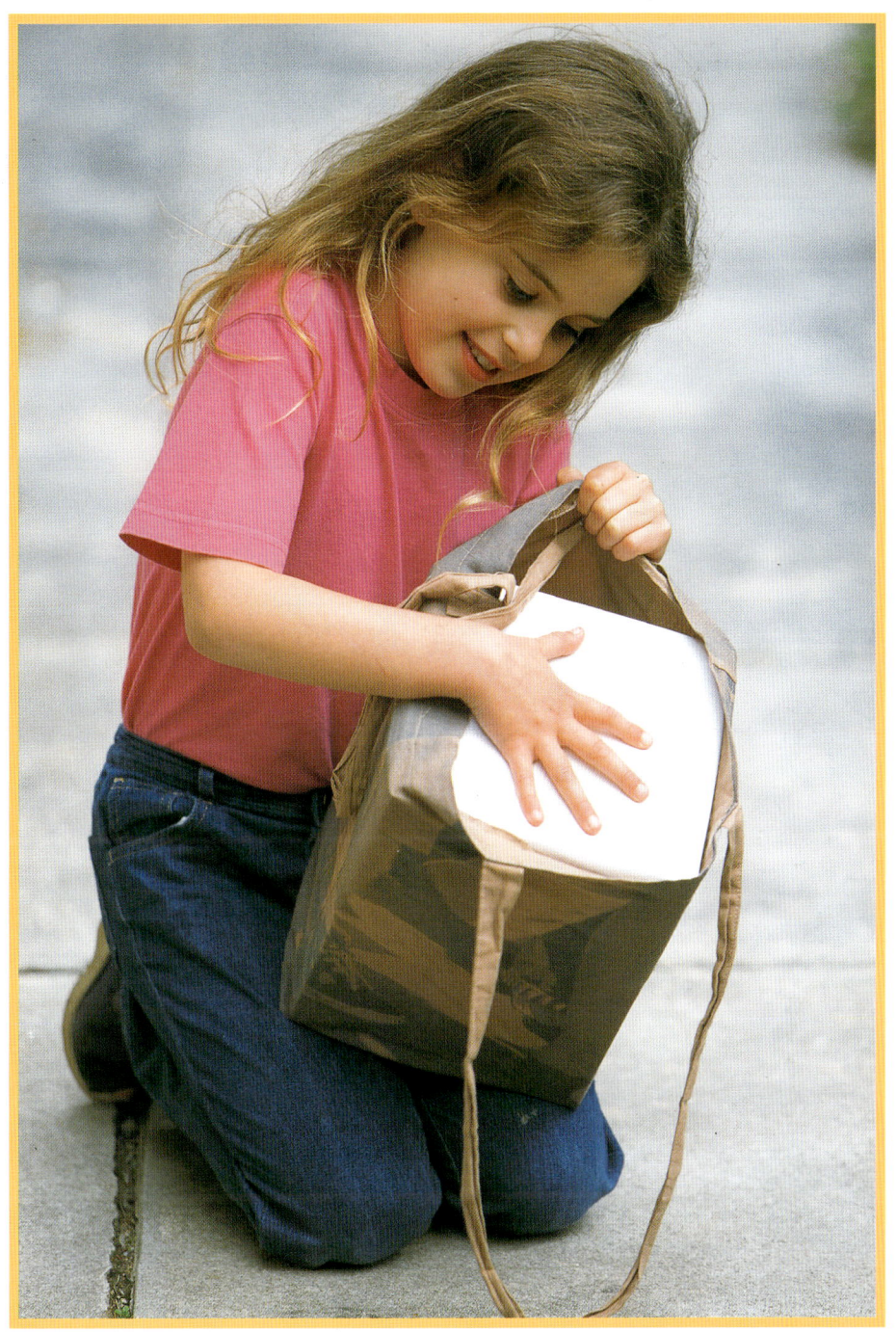

The bag is in a car.

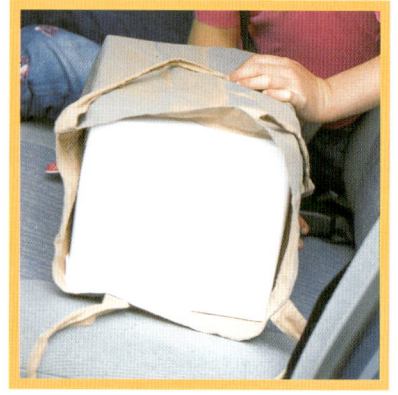

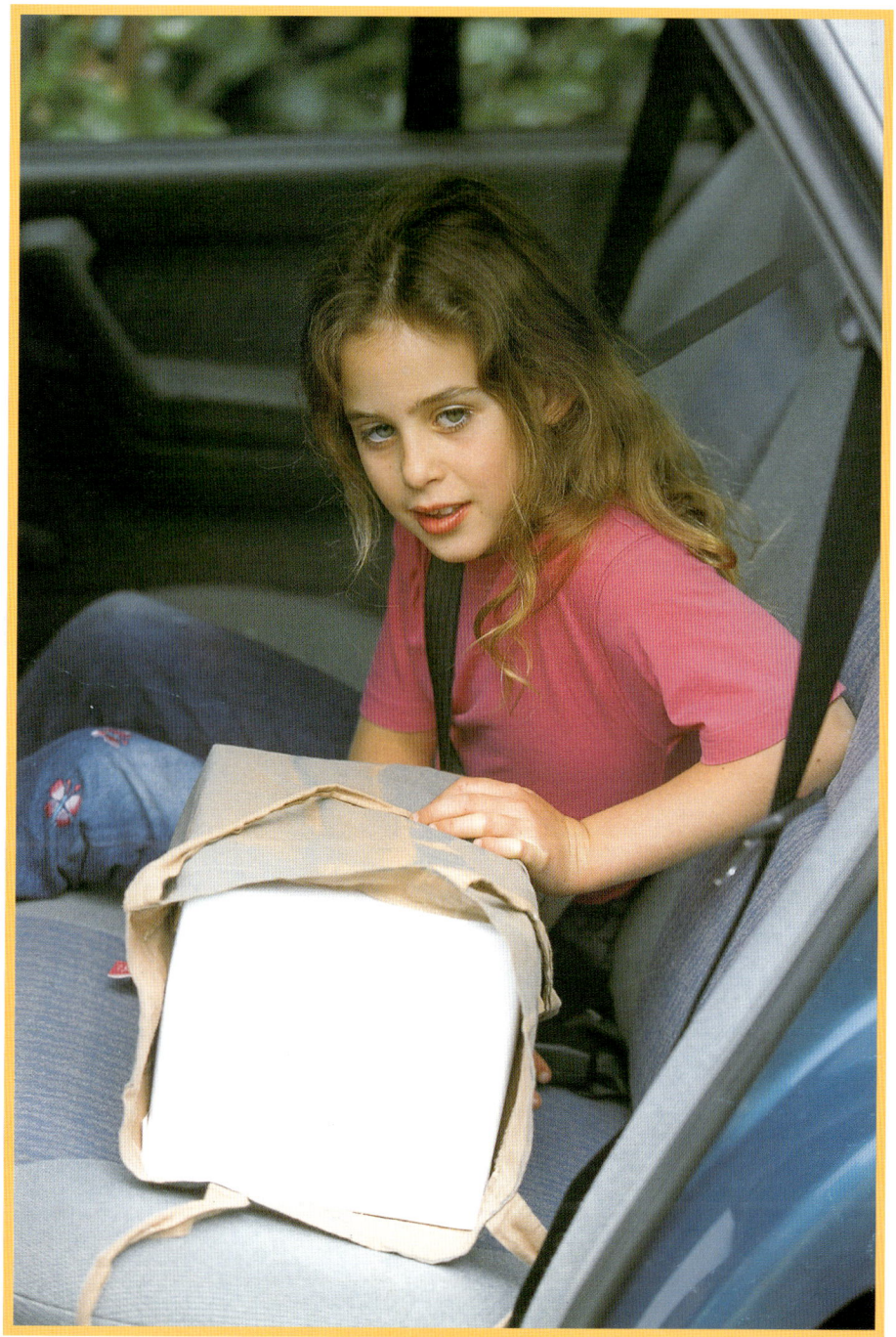

The bag is in a house.

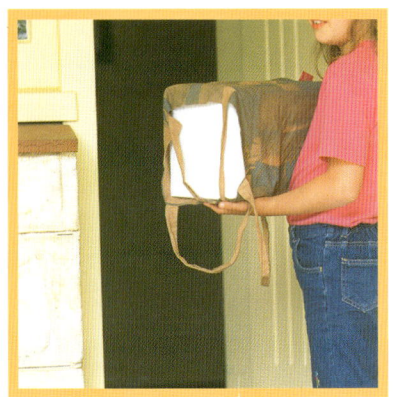

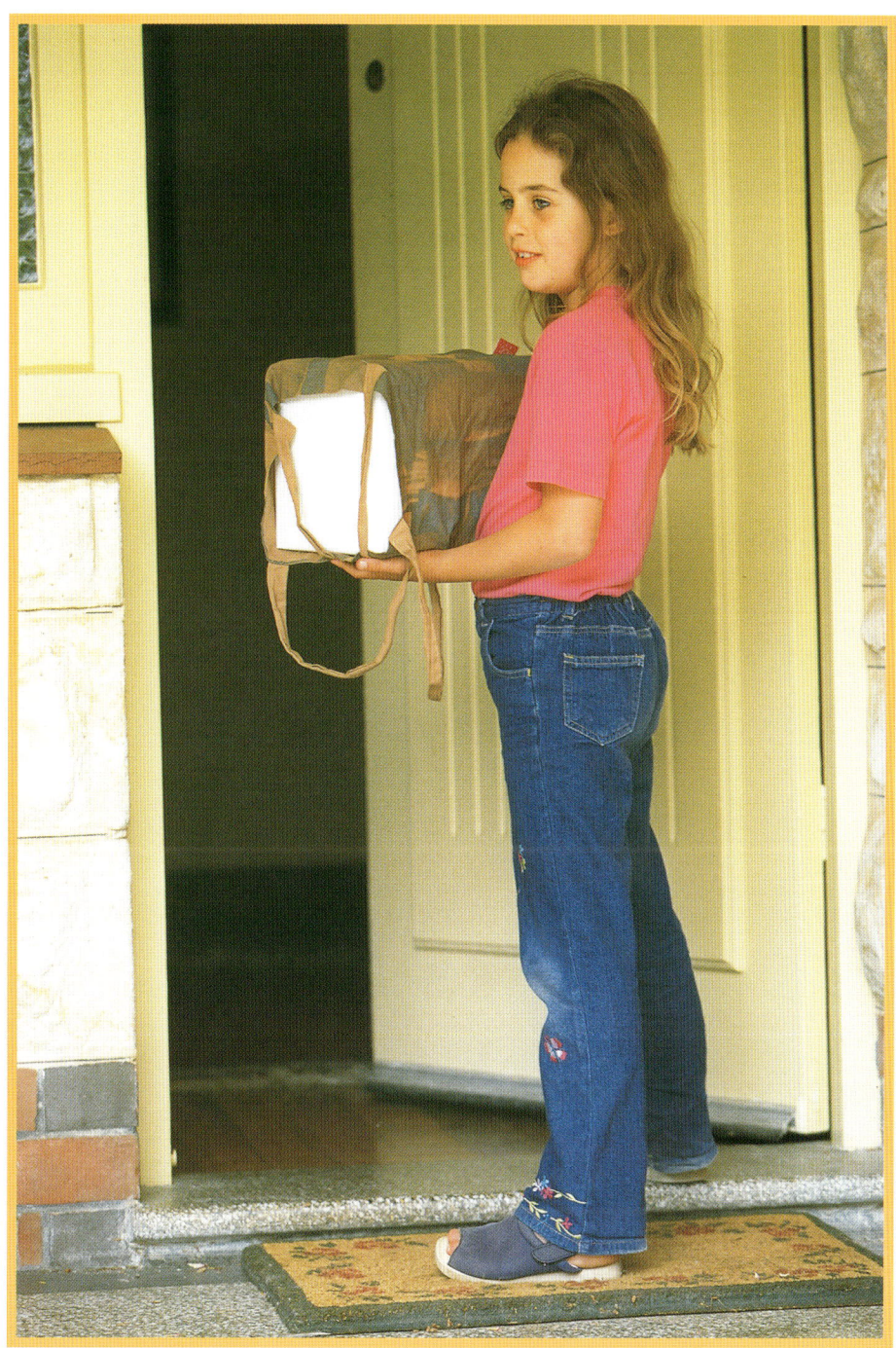

The box is out.

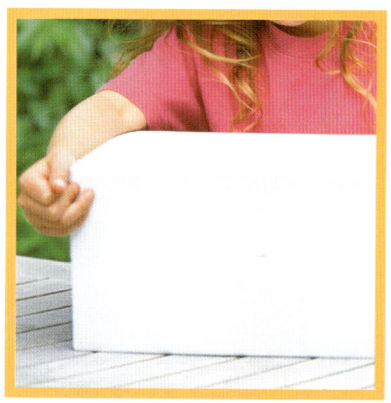

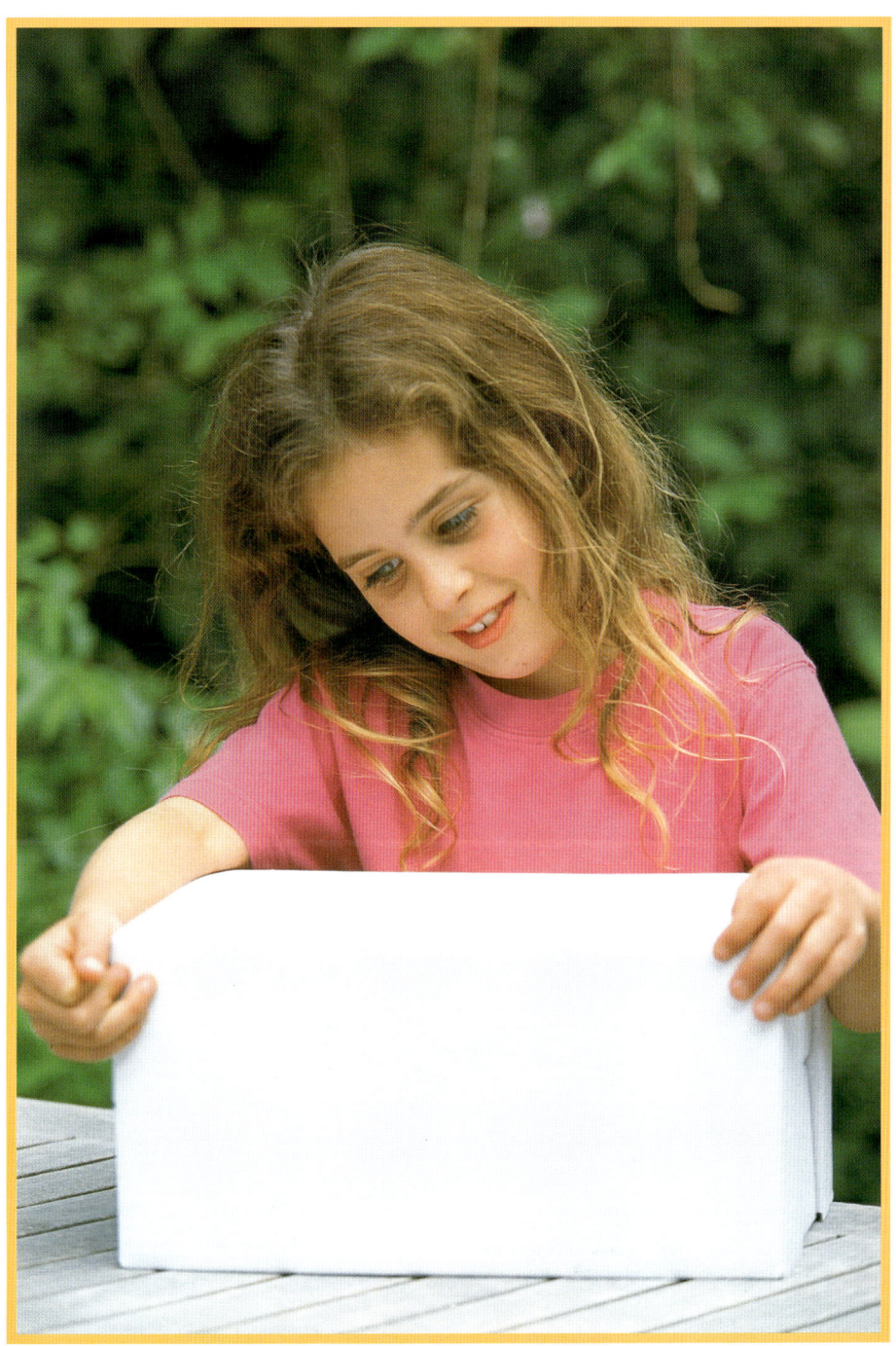

The cake is out.

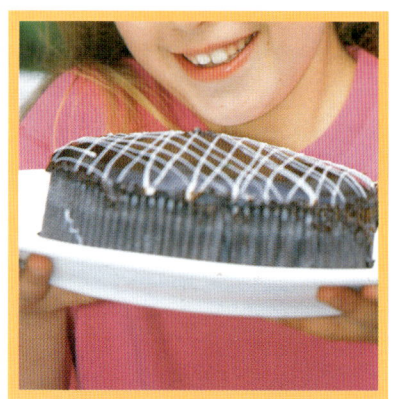

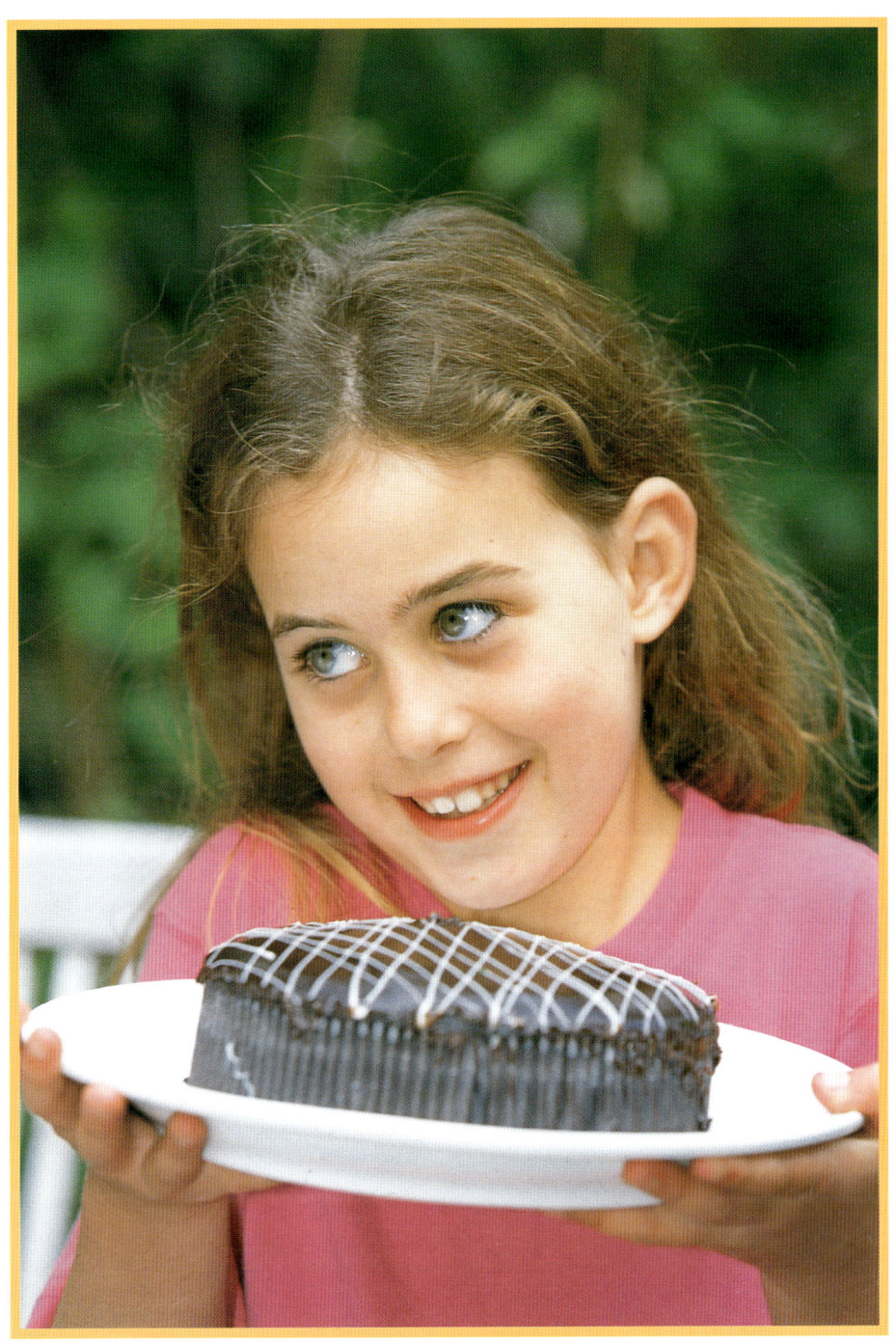

Happy birthday!

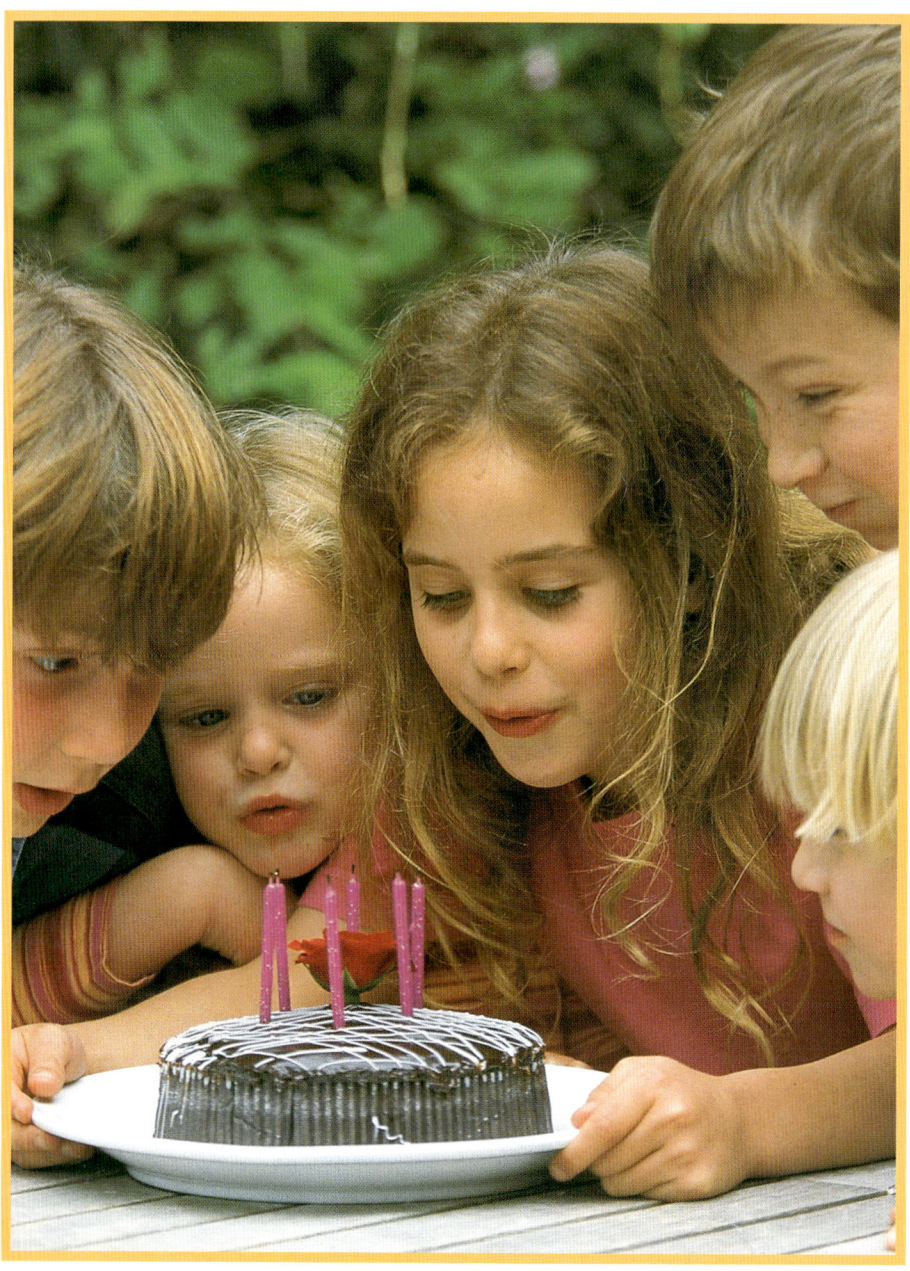